# WHAT EVERY CHRISTIAN SHOULD KNOW ABOUT

# SAME-SEX ATTRACTION

All Scripture references are from the Holman Christian Standard Bible (2004) unless otherwise indicated.

# WHAT EVERY CHRISTIAN SHOULD KNOW ABOUT

# SAME-SEX ATTRACTION

## A BIBLICAL PRIMER FOR THE LOCAL CHURCH

ROB PHILLIPS

# ACKNOWLEDGMENTS

Many thanks to Dr. Bill Victor for his scholarship, pastoral experience, and editing skills as he played a key role in the completion of this manuscript. Bill serves as elder-teaching pastor of Missio Dei Community Church in Columbia, Mo. He also serves as regional collegiate coordinator at the Missouri Baptist Convention (MBC).

In addition, I am grateful for the support and encouragement of Dr. John Yeats, executive director-treasurer of the MBC. His wide-ranging experience in all levels of denominational life provided the impetus for creating a simple, theologically sound primer for Christians desiring to be Biblically faithful and culturally relevant.

# CONTENTS

*We must draw a distinction between unwanted same-sex attraction ... and same-sex desires and behaviors.*

# 1

# NEW MCCARTHYISM?

## *Seeing same-sex attraction through a Biblical lens*

In May 2015 Ireland became the first country to legalize gay marriage by popular vote after a referendum found that 62 percent of voters favor changing the constitution to allow gay and lesbian couples to marry. At the time of this writing, 18 other nations have approved same-sex marriage, while two others – Mexico and the United States – have regional or court-directed provisions allowing same-sex couples to marry.[1]

Response to the Irish vote varied from euphoria ("It's our Berlin Wall!") to despair (a "defeat for humanity").[2] The church also is divided on the issue, with some denominations sanctioning gay marriage, others blessing same-sex unions, and still others remaining staunchly opposed to any sexual conduct outside the confines of lifelong, monogamous, heterosexual marriage.

If polls are any indication, a majority of Americans already favor same-sex marriage, and that number continues to grow. The issue of gay rights, which is not restricted to same-sex marriage, has advanced with great speed to the point where many Americans are resigned to the belief that the public celebration of homosexuality is with us to stay. No doubt, many Christians share this sense of inevitability.

Indeed, leaders of the lesbian, gay, bisexual, and transgender (LGBT) community have done a masterful job of equating gay rights with civil rights. Therefore, to oppose homosexual behavior in general, or same-sex marriage in particular, is akin to being racist. Through legal action, the media, educational initiatives, and other means, the LGBT community has sought to marginalize those who stand against the gay lifestyle on convictional, and particularly religious, grounds. Carry a Biblical worldview into the public square and you risk being labeled a right-wing extremist engaged in "New McCarthyism."[3]

At the same time, through the way we live our lives, Christians to some degree have surrendered the moral high ground. Numerous surveys show that the sexual and marital behavior of Christians does not differ significantly from that of non-Christians, meaning our conduct stands in stark contrast to what the Bible teaches about God's intent for sexuality and marriage. If Christians engage in premarital sex, adultery, pornography, and divorce about as often as non-Christians, so the argument goes, who are we to judge others?

Thankfully, God has spoken clearly in His Word. His standards of sexual purity and marital fidelity apply to all people. They reflect both His holiness and His creative intent for pleasure, security, and procreation through life-long monogamous relationships between men and women created in His image.

It's to our benefit, therefore, to revisit the issue of homosexuality through a Biblical lens – not just to know what the Bible says, but also to know what God has instructed the church to do about it. Our appraisal of any belief or action must be grounded in the Word of God. Our response should be seasoned with equal doses of conviction and compassion.

Before we begin, it's important to draw a distinction between the temptation known as unwanted same-sex attraction, which is not a sin, and same-sex desires and behaviors, which the Bible always characterizes as sinful. Every human being struggles with what the apostle Paul calls the flesh – the tarnished image of God warring against God's Word and, for the believer, against God's indwelling Spirit.

We should explore what God has to say about sex and marriage; they're both good, by the way. We should rejoice in God's creative design, earnestly pursue personal holiness, vigorously contend for the faith, and love those who experience same-sex attractions, whether they celebrate these attractions or acknowledge them as foreign to the will of God.

The world is watching. And the world is judging our response to LGBT people. Rather than wring our hands over their stunning victories in our courts, especially the court of public opinion, the church should seize this divine opportunity to speak the truth in love (Eph. 4:15). Too often we have spoken loveless truth, or surrendered truth in the name of love. Scripture calls us to embrace both truth and love.

*The first three chapters of Genesis matter because they capture the essence of creation, rebellion and redemption – the great story of the Bible.*

# 2

# DIVINE DESIGN

## *God's creative intent for sex and marriage*

The best place to begin a Biblical analysis of same-sex attraction and conduct is, well, in the beginning. Genesis 1-3 sets the stage for our study. The first three chapters of Scripture introduce us to God, reveal His eternality, instruct us in His sovereignty, suggest His triune nature, and demonstrate His power and purpose in creation. He created men and women as the crown of His creation, making them in His image and after His likeness (Gen. 1:26). He created us for relationship – with one another but most importantly with Him. He created us to rule – that is, to manage the perfectly good world He made for us and entrusted to our keeping. And He made us to reproduce. "Be fruitful, multiply, fill the earth, and subdue it," He commands Adam (Gen. 1:28).

God created people in a unique way. While He spoke the material universe into existence, and spoke the animal kingdom into being, He made Adam from the dust of the earth and breathed into his nostrils the breath of life. He then made Eve from Adam's side. This distinction should not be lost to us. Through the special creation of human beings, God demonstrates the high value He places on human life and the awesome responsibility He lays at our feet. Consider the uniquely human gifts of reason, spirituality, marriage, and everlasting life. We should keep these divinely bestowed blessings in mind when we consider sexual desires and conduct.

God created us for exclusive intimacy with Him – He shares His glory with no other god and is jealous for our full devotion to Him. He also made us for exclusive intimacy with our spouses, and gave us an expression of His creative power through procreation in the context of monogamous, life-long, heterosexual marriage.

Note that God allows Adam to discover he is alone and in need of a helper. The animals are not suitable helpers for the man – not because they lack utilitarian value, but because they are unable to help Adam carry out God's command to "fill the earth." Eve, however, can and does satisfy this role. Together, the first two human beings procreate, engaging in sexual intimacy that results in other humans who bear the image of God.

But our story takes a tragic turn in Genesis 3. Satan tempts Eve with a half-truth that makes it seem to the first couple that God is holding out on them. They disobey God, partaking of the one tree in the Garden of Eden that's off limits to them. Immediately, they experience shame. They hide from the presence of God. And they experience the curse, which includes banishment from the Garden, difficulty in childbirth, a lifetime of laboring in a hostile environment and, ultimately, death. We don't have to read far in Scripture to see how the fall of man poisons everything, including sexual intimacy, marriage, and family.

Yet God does not wash His hands of the human race. For Adam and Eve, He provides animal skins for their naked bodies, and in the process evidently teaches them about atonement – the temporary covering of sins through the substitutionary death of innocent and spotless animals. More important, He promises them redemption through Eve's "seed," who will crush the head of Satan, though the evil one will strike His heel (Gen. 3:15).

So, in the first three chapters of God's Word we see creation, rebellion, and redemption. The rest of Scripture expands on these themes. Humans become so vile, and creation so corrupted by sin, that God destroys them all, except for Noah and his family, who find salvation in a wooden ark.

By Genesis 12, God calls Abraham out of Ur and makes promises to him, including a people, land, and a global blessing. He rescues the Israelites out of captivity in Egypt and places them in the Promised Land. He gives them the Mosaic Law and the sacrificial system – one to show them God's uncompromising holiness, and the other to provide a means of atonement for sin that foreshadows the coming of the Messiah, the Lamb of God who takes away the sin of the world. God's special people – the Israelites – persistently and repeatedly rebel despite the divine call to repentance through the prophets.

And then, after the northern and southern kingdoms of God's people suffer humiliating defeat and exile – God's just punishment for sinning unrepentantly – the world seemingly goes dark for more than 400 years, until a special star hovering over Bethlehem lights the way for magi from the East to cast their eyes upon the infant King of kings. The eternal Son of God sets aside His heavenly glory and adds to His deity sinless humanity through the miracle of the virgin birth. Jesus of Nazareth lives a sinless life, performs miracles, forgives sins, receives worship, proclaims the kingdom of God – and in exchange for the humble gesture of deity becoming humanity, He is rejected, betrayed, abandoned, and crucified on a wooden cross at the hands of religious leaders who do not recognize the hour of their visitation (Luke 19:44).

Satan, at last, strikes at the heel of the promised seed of woman, resulting in His death. But in this, the greatest crime in all humanity, the seed crushes Satan's head as He bears the sin debt of all humanity, satisfies the Father's wrath, is buried, and rises triumphantly from the dead three days later. Today, seated at the Father's right hand, Jesus plunders Satan's goods, bringing into His kingdom those whom Satan once bound and blinded. He prepares a place for the redeemed, and one day He returns victoriously as the Lion of the Tribe of Judah to judge all people, to set things right, and to restore the sin-stained world to its pristine holiness, where God Himself is our God and wipes away every tear from our eyes.

The first three chapters of Genesis matter because they capture the essence of creation, rebellion, and redemption – the great story of the Bible. What does all of this have to do with human sexuality and marriage? Plenty. Consider several key truths in the opening chapters of the Bible:

1. God brilliantly designs men and women in a complementary way that enables people to help one another accomplish His creative intent to multiply and fill the earth.

2. Marriage is a pre-political institution. God establishes marriage "as the institution through which He would equip humanity to populate and cultivate His creation."[4]

3. In marriage, two become one, united in body, mind, and purpose.

4. Sexual intercourse is the only biological process that leads to procreation, implying that marriage requires gender diversity.

5. Marriage comes with the expectation of permanence.

6. The fact that the first couple sinned does not negate God's design for sexuality and marriage.

7. Marriage offers a picture of the fidelity, commitment, and love that Christ has for His church. The apostle Paul quotes both Jesus and Genesis in repeating God's intent for marriage in his letter to the Ephesians: "For this reason a man will leave his father and mother and be joined to his wife, and the two will become one flesh. This mystery is profound, but I am talking about Christ and the church" (Eph. 5:31-32).[5]

Finally, in reviewing God's design for human sexuality, it's important to note that Jesus affirms Old Testament teachings about sex and marriage. In Matthew 19, the Pharisees ask Jesus, "Is it lawful for a man to divorce his wife on any grounds?" (v. 3). The Jewish leaders want Jesus' understanding of marriage and divorce from the perspective of the Jewish law. In response, Jesus places the law and its instructions on marriage in the larger context of God's creative intent. "Haven't you read," He replies, "that He who created them in the beginning made them male and female ... For this reason a man will leave his father and mother and be joined to his wife, and the two will become one flesh? So they are no longer two, but one flesh. Therefore, what God has joined together, man must not separate" (vv. 4-6).

The Pharisees respond, "Why then did Moses command us to give divorce papers and send her away?" Jesus tells them, "Moses permitted [not commanded] you to divorce your wives because of the hardness of your hearts. But it was not like that from the beginning" (vv. 7-8).

Clearly, the Lord has not changed His reasons for creating men and women, nor has His "divine accommodation" (allowing divorce under terms of the Mosaic Law) lowered His standards for sexual purity and marriage. While the Bible is riddled with stories of adultery, polygamy, rape, prostitution, homosexuality, and other forms of sexual sin, we should not allow ourselves to become desensitized, or worse, to think that because this is the way it has almost always been, this is how it *should* be. Remember that the Bible does not endorse everything it reports. Many passages are descriptive but not prescriptive. God's command that Hosea marry a prostitute, for example, is for the purpose of prophetic illustration; it is not an endorsement of prostitution or marital infidelity.

Pastor and author Kevin DeYoung remarks that if God wanted to establish a world in which the normative marital and sexual relationship is that between persons of the opposite sex, Genesis 1-2 fits perfectly. The narrative strongly suggests what the church has almost uniformly believed and taught: that marriage is to be between one man and one woman. A different marital arrangement requires an entirely different creation account, he argues: "It's hard not to conclude from a straightforward reading of Genesis 1-2 that the divine design for sexual intimacy is not any combination of persons, or even any type of two persons coming together, but one man becoming one flesh with one woman."[6]

DeYoung notes that there are at least five reasons we are right to think that Genesis 1-2 establishes God's design for marriage and that this design requires one man and one woman:

1. The way in which the woman was created indicates that she is the man's divinely designed complement.

2. The nature of the one-flesh union presupposes two persons of the opposite sex.

3. Only two persons of the opposite sex can fulfill the procreative purposes of marriage.

4. Jesus reinforces the normativity of the Genesis account.

5. The redemptive-historical significance of marriage as a divine symbol in the Bible only works if the marital couple is a complementary pair.[7]

As we explore the Bible's treatment of same-sex conduct, it helps to keep in mind the creation-rebellion-redemption story of Genesis 1-3, repeated and expanded throughout the rest of Scripture. We live in a sinful and fallen world. It was not always this way. And it will not always be this way. Until our Redeemer returns to set things right, we should set our own houses in order, obeying His command to "be alert, because you don't know either the day or the hour" (Matt. 25:13). What we believe and how we live matters – not only to us, but to our friends struggling with same-sex attraction. We should embrace and proclaim God's creative intent for sexuality and marriage – but humbly, graciously, and lovingly, lest we be tempted as well (Gal. 6:1).[8]

*The Bible speaks positively of loving, monogomous, lifelong relationships between a man and a woman, but never of two women or two men.*

# 3

# SIX KEY PASSAGES

*And why they matter*

While the whole of Scripture argues against all forms of sexual immorality, the following six passages speak directly to the issue of same-sex conduct. Several English versions are compared to highlight differences in translation.

## GENESIS 19:5

They [the men of Sodom] called out to Lot and said, "Where are the men who came to you tonight? Send them out to us so we can **have sex with them!**" (HCSB)

- "... that we may **know them.**" (KJV)
- "... that we may **have relations with them.**" (NASB)
- "... that we can **have sex with them.**" (NIV)
- "... that we may **know them.**" (ESV)

### *Summary*

God destroys the ancient cities of Sodom and Gomorrah because of the people's wickedness, expressed most egregiously in their homosexual behavior. Jews and Christians traditionally have understood the story of Sodom and Gomorrah to speak directly to the issue of homosexuality – revisionist explanations of this passage notwithstanding.

Gen. 13:13 tells us, "Now the men of Sodom were evil, sinning greatly against the Lord." When two angels and the Lord Himself visit Lot, the Lord says, "The outcry against Sodom and Gomorrah is immense, and their sin is extremely serious" (Gen. 18:20). Their sin clearly is homosexual behavior, for they surround Lot's house and demand that his three guests be given to them so they may "have sex with them" (Gen. 19:5). Lot implores the men, "Don't do this evil, my brothers" (v. 7), and he takes the extraordinary step of offering his two virgin daughters to them if they only abandon their intent for the three guests under Lot's roof.

Other references to these two cities cast them in the light of grievous, unrepentant sin. Jude 7, for example, refers to their behavior as "sexual immorality" and "perversions," and 2 Peter 2:7 describes "the unrestrained behavior of the immoral." The depiction of the "men" of Sodom surrounding Lot's house shows that the entire populace is corrupt. The "whole population" – young and old, from every quarter – is engaged in this immoral practice (Gen. 19:4). For this sin, the Lord destroys the cities in an act of divine judgment.

## *Challenges*

The most common objection to the plain reading of the text is the interpretation that the sin of Sodom is primarily inhospitality, not same-sex behavior. Proponents of this view often cite Ezek. 16:48-49 to say that the sin of the Sodomites is their refusal to take in needy travelers. No doubt the men of Sodom are an inhospitable bunch, but reading the next verse changes the perspective:

"They were haughty and did detestable things before Me, so I removed them when I saw this" (v. 50). The word "detestable" – or "abomination" in other translations – brings us back to Leviticus, specifically Lev. 18:22 and Lev. 20:13, where homosexual conduct is in view.

Another challenge is that the use of the word *yada* – translated "know" in the KJV and ESV – does not refer to homosexual conduct. It's true that the word *yada* appears numerous times in the Bible and normally refers to knowing factual information, but at times *yada* plainly means to know someone intimately in a sexual fashion.

For example, in Gen. 4:1 Adam "knew Eve his wife; and she conceived ..." (KJV). Further, a look at Judges 19:22-25 offers a close parallel to the story of Lot in Sodom. Certain "perverted men of the city" surround the home where two guests have been taken in, demanding, "Bring out the man who came to your house so we can have sex (*yada*) with him!" (v. 22). The homeowner describes their intent as "evil" and "horrible" (v. 23), and he offers his virgin daughter and the guest's concubine in exchange. The men take the concubine, rape (*yada*) her and abuse her all night (v. 25).

The context determines the correct understanding of the word *yada*.

A third challenge is that Jesus mentions Sodom and Gomorrah but does not connect the cities with homosexuality. It's true that in Matt. 10:14-15, as Jesus commissions the 12 disciples, He does not specifically refer to any sin for which the residents of the cities are guilty. His exact words are: "If anyone will not welcome you or listen to your words, shake the dust off your feet when you leave that house or town. I assure you: It will be more tolerable on the day of judgment for the land of Sodom and Gomorrah than for that town."

As James White and Jeffrey Niell explain, "Sodom's judgment had become axiomatic for the fullest outpouring of God's wrath throughout the Old Testament.... The issue is that these cities will be held accountable to God for their grievous sins. And the comparison is that it will be more tolerable for Sodom and Gomorrah in that day than for those cities that had experienced the visitation of the very apostles of the incarnate Lord, but refused their message of repentance and faith."[9]

A final challenge is that the story of Sodom and Gomorrah is not germane to the same-sex debate because it does not address loving, monogamous relationships. It only rails against homosexual gang rape and violence. Even if that were the case, it begs the question of what the Bible says, if anything, about loving, monogamous same-sex relationships. Again, White and Niell are helpful: "To call a relationship 'loving' in a Biblical sense means it is in accordance with God's will and is fulfilling His purpose, resulting in His glory."[10] The Bible speaks positively of loving, monogamous, lifelong relationships between a man and a woman, but never of two women or two men.

## LEVITICUS 18:22 AND 20:13

**Lev. 18:22** - You are not to sleep with a **man** as with a **woman**; it is **detestable**. (HCSB)

- Thou shalt not lie with **mankind**, as with **womankind**: it is **abomination**. (KJV)

- You shall not lie with a **male** as one lies with a **female**; it is an **abomination**. (NASB)
- Do not have sexual relations with a **man** as one does with a **woman**; that is **detestable**. (NIV)
- You shall not lie with a **male** as with a **woman**; it is an **abomination**. (ESV)

**Lev. 20:13** - If a man **sleeps with a man as with a woman,** they have both committed **an abomination**. They must be put to death; their blood is on their own hands. (HCSB)

- If a man also **lie with mankind, as he lieth with a woman**, both of them have committed **an abomination** ... (KJV)
- If there is a **man who lies with a male as those who lie with a woman**, both of them have committed a **detestable act** ... (NASB)
- If a man has **sexual relations with a man as one does with a woman**, both of them have done what is **detestable** ... (NIV)
- If a man **lies with a male as with a woman**, both of them have committed **an abomination** ... (ESV)

## *Summary*

These verses are part of the Holiness Code (Leviticus 17-26) dealing with laws, sacrifices, and purity regulations that distinguish the Hebrews from the idolatrous nations surrounding them. The code prohibits sowing a field with two kinds of seeds, wearing a garment made of two kinds of materials, and other activities that seem foreign to 21st Century readers. This leads some critics to conclude that the passages on homosexual behavior also are meant only for Hebrews living in the ancient Near East.

However, there are good reasons to understand these prohibitions as an expression of God's unchanging moral will. Kevin DeYoung offers six reasons not to set aside Lev. 18:22 and 20:13:

1. No disciple of Jesus should start with the presumption that the Mosaic commands are largely irrelevant. Jesus Himself insisted that He did not come to abolish the tiniest speck from the Law (Matt. 5:17-18).

2. There is no indication in the New Testament that Leviticus should be treated as particularly obscure or peripheral. The sexual ethic of the Old Testament was not abrogated like the sacrificial system, but carried forward into the early church. The law is good if one uses it lawfully (1 Tim. 1:8).

3. Paul's term for "men who practice homosexuality" (1 Cor. 6:9; 1 Tim.1:10) is derived from two words – *arsen* (man) and *koite* (bed) – found in Lev. 18:22 and 20:13 (Septuagint).

4. Leviticus uses strong language in denouncing homosexual behavior, calling it "an abomination." Outside of Leviticus, the Hebrew word *to'ebah* appears 43 times in Ezekiel and 68 times in the rest of the Old Testament, usually with respect to especially grievous sins. We cannot reduce the word to a mere social taboo or ritual uncleanness.

5. The reference to a woman's menstrual period (18:19; 20:18) should not call into question the rest of the sexual ethic described in Leviticus 18 and 20. For starters, there is a clear progression in both chapters

of sexual sin deviating in increasing measure from the design of male-female monogamy. Menstruation was not a sin but a matter of ritual uncleanness. But with the coming of Christ, the entire system that required ritual cleanness was removed.

6. Apart from the question of sex during menstruation, the New Testament affirms the sexual ethic of Leviticus 18 and 20.[11]

The prohibitions of Leviticus 18 and 20 are against behavior that is contrary to God's creative intent for sexuality. Further, the New Testament writers repeat the Levitical prohibitions against same-sex behavior (Rom. 1:26-27; 1 Cor. 6:9-11; 1 Tim. 1:8-11). Not a single passage in the Old or New Testaments depicts homosexual conduct in a positive light.

## *Challenges*

One common objection is that these passages speak negatively of homosexual conduct that violates the gender roles appropriate to a patriarchal society because the act reduces the passive partner to the status of a woman. If this were the case, however, the active partner would be guiltier than the passive partner. Yet the Bible holds both parties equally to blame and subscribes the same punishment for both persons.

Another argument is that homosexual relations in the ancient Near East often were between social unequals – for example, a master and his slave or a man and a boy. Since this type of behavior is no longer considered appropriate in most cultures, the prohibition in Leviticus does not apply. However, Lev. 18:22 and Lev. 20:13 do not restrict the type of homosexual behavior that

God considers an abomination; all forms of same-sex conduct are prohibited.

Yet another contention is that these verses decry violent behavior such as same-sex rape or homosexual behavior associated with idolatry like cult prostitution. They say nothing about same-sex conduct between "loving" and "committed" people. But the Hebrew word *zakar* always involves the male gender, whether translated "man," "male," or "mankind," thus meaning that all forms of male-male sexual activity are included in the prohibition. Further, Leviticus 18 condemns adultery, child sacrifice, and prostitution, which are wrong apart from any connection with cult prostitution. And Leviticus 20 places homosexuality between incest and bestiality, which have no direct link to idolatry. Finally, when the Lord wants to condemn cult prostitution, He does it clearly, as in Deut. 23:17.

Some, like Rabbi Jacob Milgrom, contend that the Levitical prohibitions against same-sex conduct applied only to the Jews, and only to non-Jews if they resided in the Holy Land. James White and Jeffrey Niell counter: "Essentially, Milgrom is arguing that homosexuality was wrong for an Egyptian if he resided in Judah, but it was not wrong if he lived in Egypt or Macedonia." Referring to this position as "geographical morality," the authors add, "Is it acceptable for a Jew to be a homosexual in New York, Denver, or Uganda, but not in Bethlehem?"[12]

Then, of course, come the arguments that Christians today selectively promote the portions of Leviticus that suit them – such as the commands against same-sex behavior – but ignore the parts dealing with dietary restrictions, agricultural practices, and the knitting of garments. In other words, if Christians today don't observe all the Levitical prescriptions, they have no right to condemn homosexual behavior.

So, why don't we observe the dietary laws? Because Jesus removed them and declared all foods clean (Mark 7:19). Further, the laws about the separation of fabrics and seed were to distinguish the Hebrews from their neighbors; nowhere were the nations surrounding Israel punished for these behaviors, meaning they were specific to the Hebrews. In stark contrast, nowhere does Scripture set aside its prohibition against homosexual behavior.

Christian author Paul Copan goes further in helping us understand God's intentions behind the Bible's seeming "ubiquitous weirdness." While His laws for the Israelites appear to have covered every aspect of life – food laws, clothing laws, planting laws, civil laws, laws regarding marriage and sexual relations – these were not intended to be exhaustive, or necessarily permanent in all cases. Rather, "they were to be viewed first as visible reminders to live as God's holy people in every area of life. There wasn't any division between the sacred and the secular, between the holy and the profane. God was concerned about holiness in all things – the major and the minor, the significant and the mundane. In such legislation, Israel was being reminded that she was different, a holy people set apart to serve God."[13]

Copan notes that God gives the Israelites certain actions to carry out as a way of *symbolically* telling them not to get mixed in with the false ways of the nations. "Israel 'wore' certain badges of holy distinction that separated them from the morally and theologically corrupted nations surrounding them; they were not to get 'mixed in' with those nations' mind-set and behavior." For example, the prohibition against two kinds of seed in the same field "may refer to a Canaanite magical practice of the 'wedding' of different seeds to conjure up fertile crops."[14]

## ROMANS 1:26-27

This is why God delivered them over to **degrading passions**. For even their females exchanged natural sexual intercourse for what is **unnatural**. The males in the same way also left natural sexual intercourse with females and were inflamed in their lust for one another. Males committed **shameless acts** with males and received in their own persons the appropriate penalty for their **perversion**. (HCSB)

- For this cause God gave them up unto **vile affections**: for even their women did change the natural use into that which is **against nature**: And likewise also the men, leaving the natural use of the woman, burned in their lust one toward another; men with men **working that which is unseemly**, and receiving in themselves that recompense of their **error** which was meet. (KJV)
- For this reason God gave them over to **degrading passions**; for their women exchanged the natural function for that which is **unnatural**, and in the same way also the men abandoned the natural function of the woman and burned in their desire toward one another, men with men committing **indecent acts** and receiving in their own persons the due penalty of their **error**. (NASB)
- Because of this, God gave them over to **shameful lusts**. Even their women exchanged natural sexual relations for **unnatural** ones. In the same way the men also abandoned natural relations with women and were inflamed with lust for one another. Men committed **shameful acts** with other men, and received in themselves the due penalty for their **error**. (NIV)

- For this reason God gave them up to **dishonorable passions**. For their women exchanged natural relations for those that are **contrary to nature**; and the men likewise gave up natural relations with women and were consumed with passion for one another, men committing **shameless acts** with men and receiving in themselves the due penalty for their error. (ESV)

## *Summary*

Of all Biblical texts in the same-sex debate, Rom. 1:26-27 appears to be the most common and most-often cited. Before Paul may proclaim the good news of salvation by grace through faith, he must establish the human need for this divine gift, and he does so in the first two and a half chapters by laying out his case for the sinfulness of mankind.

The apostle singles out homosexuality in Rom. 1:26-27 to illustrate the descending spiral of depravity that befalls those who refuse to acknowledge God's lordship over their lives. God has revealed Himself to all people – including his eternal power and divine nature – in creation and conscience, leaving people without an excuse for rejecting Him in favor of idolatry and ungodly passions (Rom. 1:18-23). No one may stand before Christ on judgment day and proclaim he or she didn't know there was a divine designer or a divine moral lawgiver.

Meanwhile, as people reject the revelation of God and His holy standards, He allows them to descend a spiral staircase into outer darkness as they prefer other gods, profess themselves wiser than their Creator, and embrace the fleshly passions borne of unbelief. Three times in Romans 1 Paul writes that "God delivered them over" – in "the cravings of their hearts," "to degrading passions," and "to a worthless mind to do what is morally wrong." These are judicial acts on God's part in which essentially He says, "Have it your way, but take note that your sins will consume you."

Verses 26-27 form a single thought, connected by the introductory words, "This is why God delivered them over ..." These verses are not isolated from the rest of Romans 1 but fit perfectly within the context of Paul's theme of human depravity. God delivers them over to "degrading passions" (HCSB), "vile affections" (KJV), and "shameful lusts" (NIV). However the phrase is translated, it refers to desires and behaviors that dishonor God and degrade human dignity.

Paul then offers a fitting example of these behaviors, writing first about lesbianism and then male homosexuality. Females "exchanged natural sexual intercourse for what is unnatural," meaning they willfully sought same-sex relations in violation of God's revealed creative intent. Further, "males in the same way also left natural sexual intercourse with females and were inflamed in their lust for one another," illustrating once again their conscious rebellion against God and His holy standards as revealed in nature.

Paul ends this verse by calling homosexual conduct "shameless acts" and pointing out that these acts result in "the appropriate penalty for their perversion." This penalty may include both temporal consequences of the gay lifestyle – higher than normal levels of certain physical illnesses, mental and emotional trauma, etc.[15] – and everlasting consequences for those who reject divine revelation and refuse to repent. Persons who land on Romans 1 are encouraged to read on, for Paul introduces the remedy for human depravity – the gift of God, which is eternal life in Christ Jesus our Lord (Rom. 6:23).

## *Challenges*

One objection is that Paul is ignorant of the reality of sexual orientation. He has no idea that some people are naturally attracted to people of the same sex. Therefore, he misunderstands sexual orientation, which is widely understood and accepted today.

Responding to this appeal, it's important to understand that this argument implicates the Holy Spirit, who inspired Scripture. If Paul does not understand the subject about which he is writing, then the Spirit either is ignorant of modern concepts of sexuality or is lax by not enlightening Paul. If the modern concept of sexual orientation is to be taken as fact, then the Bible cannot be trusted to reveal what it means to be human, made in God's image, and guilty of sin as God defines it. If God does not know what it means to be gay in the 21st Century, what else does He not know?

The assumption that Paul is unaware of "sexual orientation" is faulty. The American Psychological Association defines sexual orientation as "an enduring pattern of emotional, romantic and/or sexual attractions to men, women or both sexes."[16] Notice that orientation involves a person's enduring sexual attractions, and sexual attraction is virtually synonymous with desire. Thus sexual orientation is a person's persistent pattern of sexual attraction / desire toward either or both sexes.

There is no reason to believe that Paul is not fully aware of human attractions and desires, no matter how sinful they are. To expand on this a little, it's good to note that Paul hails from Tarsus, a major city in the Roman Empire. He is well trained, widely read, and familiar with Roman and Greek culture. Therefore, it's implausible to assert that he knew nothing of people who professed homosexuality as their "orientation." *Plato's Symposium*, written centuries before Paul's letter to the Romans, shows that those in ancient cultures are well aware of a wide range of homosexual behavior, even if they don't use the word "orientation."

Look at Paul's words: He refers to "degrading passions" or attractions/desires, and he describes those who are "inflamed in their lust for one another." As Denny Burk writes, "Sexual desire that fixates on the same sex is sinful, and that is why God's judgment rightly falls on both desires and actions. Again, the issue Paul addresses is not merely sexual behavior but also same-sex attraction."[17]

A second argument is that Paul is only condemning oppressive, pederastic, or socially mixed same-sex acts. This is what Paul means by "unnatural."

In response, we should point out numerous linguistic links between Rom. 1:26-27 and the creation narratives of Genesis 1-2. For example, Paul's use of the relatively unusual words *thelys* for females and *arsen* for males strongly suggests he is relying on the creation account of Genesis 1 where the same two words are employed in the Septuagint, the Greek translation of the Old Testament. These two terms highlight the sexual differences between males and females and suggest that homosexual relationships violate God's creative intent. For Paul, it seems clear that "unnatural" means homosexual conduct that goes against God's creative design.

A third argument is that "unnatural" refers to heterosexuals who go beyond their natural bounds and explore homosexuality. This is a subtle way of twisting Paul's words into an affirmation of homosexual behavior that is "natural to me." But to engage in *eisegesis* – or reading a particular meaning into the text – is to place depraved human thinking above God's plainly revealed

Word. The entire context of Romans 1 argues against this sort of reasoning. In fact, to say homosexuality is "natural to me" and therefore good is to make Paul's point that rejecting God's revelation in creation and conscience results in nonsensical thinking and darkened reasoning.

There are other, less common, objections to the evangelical understanding of Rom. 1:26-27, including: (a) the view that the sinners mentioned in this passage are idolaters who engage in homosexual behavior as a way of denying the existence of God, therefore "Christian homosexuals" are not in view here; (b) the argument that Paul limits his remarks to the social and geographical context of his day; and (c) the contention that Paul is speaking only of Jewish purity laws, thus making the passage irrelevant in today's enlightened society.

We may respond by noting: (a) the whole of Scripture argues against the idea of a "Christian homosexual" – that is, one who embraces the mutually exclusive concepts of faith in Christ and unrepentant behavior that Scripture always calls sinful; (b) the context of Romans 1 makes it clear that Paul is writing about desires and behaviors that run contrary to God's revealed standards, which are unchanging; and (c) those who hold this view are acknowledging that the Hebrew Scriptures do indeed condemn homosexual behavior; further, Paul's repeated use of universal terms to describe humanity's rejection of God's self-revelation argue in favor of a wide application.

A final thought on this passage in Romans: As Richard B. Hays points out, we cannot read the judgments against unrighteous behavior apart from the rest of the letter of Romans with its message of grace and hope through the cross of Christ. The struggle may not be easy, but Christians have been set free from the power of sin through Christ's death, and we must continue to struggle to live faithfully in the present.[18]

## 1 CORINTHIANS 6:9-10 AND 1 TIMOTHY 1:9-11

**1 Cor. 6:9-10** - Do you not know that the unjust will not inherit God's kingdom? Do not be deceived: no sexually immoral people, idolaters, adulterers, **male prostitutes, homosexuals**, thieves, greedy people, drunkards, revilers, or swindlers will inherit God's kingdom. (HCSB)

- Know ye not that the unrighteous shall not inherit the kingdom of God? Be not deceived: neither fornicators, nor idolaters, nor adulterers, nor **effeminate**, nor **abusers of themselves with mankind** ... (KJV)
- Or do you not know that the unrighteous will not inherit the kingdom of God? Do not be deceived; neither fornicators, nor idolaters, nor adulterers, nor **effeminate**, nor **homosexuals** ... (NASB)
- Or do you not know that wrongdoers will not inherit the kingdom of God? Do not be deceived: Neither the sexually immoral nor idolaters nor adulterers nor **men who have sex with men** ... (NIV)
- Or do you not know that the unrighteous will not inherit the kingdom of God? Do not be deceived: neither the sexually immoral, nor idolaters, nor adulterers, nor men who **practice homosexuality** ... (ESV)

**1 Tim. 1:9-11** - We know that the law is not meant for a righteous person, but for the lawless and rebellious, for the ungodly and sinful, for the unholy and irreverent, for those who kill their fathers and mothers, for murderers, for **the sexually immoral and homosexuals**, for kidnappers, liars, perjurers, and for whatever else is contrary to the sound teaching based on the glorious gospel of the blessed God that was entrusted to me. (HCSB)

- … For **whoremongers, for them that defile themselves with mankind** … (KJV)
- … and **immoral men and homosexuals** … (NASB)
- … for **the sexually immoral**, for those **practicing homosexuality** … (NIV)
- … for … **the sexually immoral, men who practice homosexuality** … (ESV)

## *Summary*

These two passages address moral issues facing the congregation at Corinth and in Timothy's ministry. Corinth in particular is known for its sexual sins and gross immorality, due in part to the presence of pagan worship that features temple prostitution. Paul, who spent 18 months in Corinth, begins 1 Cor. 6:9 with the words, "Do you not know …" And he follows up with, "Do not be deceived …"

The apostle is restating what he has taught them before: The kingdom of God is a kingdom of righteousness. Seated on the throne is a righteous King. Those who remain in opposition to the righteous King have excluded themselves from citizenship in His kingdom. Paul also warns of the danger of false teachers who come into the church and deceive the followers of Jesus into believing that certain sinful behaviors should be accepted – perhaps even celebrated.

It's important to note that the only sin listed in 1 Cor. 6:9-10 that is not also listed in Leviticus chapters 18-20 is drunkenness. This supports the idea that Paul is linking this passage to Leviticus. This becomes even clearer when we look at the Greek word *arsenokoites*, a word not found in Greek literature prior to Paul's writings. Paul, the apostle to the Gentiles, is well familiar with the Septuagint (also known as the LXX), the Greek translation of the Old Testament. Where the LXX differs from the Hebrew text, Paul goes with the LXX, quite possibly because he knows his audience is more familiar with that version.

Why is this important? Because when we get to the terms used in the LXX at Lev. 18:22 and Lev. 20:13, we find the words *arsenos* (male) and *koiten* (to lie with sexually, have intercourse). The term "homosexuals" in 1 Cor. 6:9 is made up of these two terms: *arsenos* and *koiten*, thus *arsenokoites*. Paul may have picked up this word from rabbinic discussions of homosexuality, or he may have coined it himself. In any case, Paul's use of this unique word ties 1 Cor. 6:9-10 and 1 Tim. 1:9-11 with the commands against homosexual behavior found in Leviticus 18 and 20. Further, we should remember that the prohibition of homosexual behavior in Leviticus is not restricted to prostitution, pederasty, or any other category of homosexuality. It condemns all forms of same-sex immorality.

And yet there is good news. Some at Corinth have been rescued from immoral behavior by the saving power of Jesus Christ. 1 Cor. 6:11 reads, "Some of you were like this; but you were washed, you were sanctified, you were justified in the name of the Lord Jesus Christ and by the Spirit of our God." Paul is not writing to "gay Christians;" he is addressing those once trapped in homosexual lust and conduct but now transformed through the regenerating, justifying, and sanctifying work of God.

Change is possible – not necessarily instantaneous or easy. But when a person entrusts his life to Jesus, he is washed – regenerated, or born of the Spirit, given a new life. He also is *declared* righteous through the sovereign act of justification – and thereby acquitted of the penalty of all sins – and then *made* righteous over the course of his life as the indwelling Spirit sanctifies him, or conforms him to the image of Christ.

In writing to Timothy and Titus, Paul expresses his deep concern for the next generation of Christian leaders. He has invested himself deeply in their lives and writes to exhort them to remain faithful in the face of withering opposition. In his first letter to Timothy, Paul reminds his beloved young friend that while salvation is not attained through the Law, the Law nevertheless serves a proper purpose in exposing human sinfulness.

In 1 Tim. 1:9-11, Paul identifies three categories of sinners: the lawless and rebellious, the ungodly and sinful, and the unholy and irreverent. He then lists specific types of sinners that fall under these headings, including "the sexually immoral and homosexuals." The word "homosexuals" in Greek is *arsenokoites*, which we encountered in 1 Cor. 6:9-10. Paul refers to homosexuals as those for whom the Law is intended, thereby tying this passage to Leviticus. Since the prohibitions in Leviticus are well known, and because Timothy no doubt is aware of Paul's previous teachings on the subject, there is no need for Paul to elaborate in this passage.

In short, Paul's writings to the church at Corinth and to Timothy address the issue of homosexual conduct. Paul links these passages to Leviticus and thus condemns all forms of same-sex behavior. He also leaves us with hope: Through His finished work on the cross, Jesus has paid the debt for these sins and invites us to repent and believe in Him for forgiveness and life-changing transformation. Because of Jesus, some who formerly engaged in same-sex behavior may now joyously declare that they have been washed, sanctified, and justified in the name of the Lord Jesus Christ and by the Spirit of our God.

## *Challenges*

One argument is that English translations fail to rightly capture the meaning of the Greek term *arsenokoites*, normally translated "homosexuals" or "those who practice homosexuality." A more accurate understanding, it is said, is excessive lust and pederasty (same-sex relations between a man and a boy), or male prostitution. These sexual activities dominate the Greco-Roman context in which Paul lived.

In response, we should note that the term *arsenokoites* appears nowhere else in Greek literature until Paul coins the term here, according to Denny Burk, professor of Biblical studies at Boyce College and author of *What Is the Meaning of Sex?*[19] There are other words for homosexual behavior, but Paul chooses not to use them. Rather, he coins a term that derives from the Greek translation of Lev. 20:13, *arsenos koiten*, thus tying 1 Cor. 6:9-10 and 1 Tim. 1:9-11 with Leviticus.

Another argument is that Paul condemns *abuses* of homosexuality, not same-sex activity altogether. Since he lists homosexuality along with other abuses of legitimate activities – for example, sexual immorality as an abuse of loving, monogamous relationships – it is the *misuse* of homosexuality, not homosexuality itself, that is the issue.

In response, it should first be noted that the objection assumes there is some form of acceptable same-sex behavior; but as we've seen throughout this study, the Bible nowhere condones same-sex conduct of any kind. Further, we should point out that Paul offers a list of behaviors that are sinful in themselves – sexual immorality, idolatry, adultery, etc. – and homosexuality is part of that list.

Finally, we should ask: Is there some degree of sexual immorality that God finds acceptable? Certain kinds of idolatry? Adultery? May I excuse theft if I argue that I was born with a natural tendency to take things that don't belong to me? When we carry this argument to its logical conclusion, we see that Paul makes no exceptions for any form of homosexual conduct.

*We must live as a community of believers that embraces sinners as Jesus did - demonstrating His humility and sacrificial love and, simultaneously, His divine righteousness.*

# 4

# THE CLARITY OF SCRIPTURE

*Seven key truths*

As we explore the Bible's teachings on homosexuality, at least seven truths emerge.

**1. The Bible condemns all forms of sexual behavior outside the bonds of heterosexual, monogamous, life-long marriage.** Homosexuality is not a special class of sin that makes it any more or less an act of rebellion against God than premarital sex, adultery, polygamy, polyandry, pornography, or other sexual sins. We do injustice to God's Word, and to those struggling with same-sex attraction, when we make homosexual conduct a special class of sin.

**2. God has spoken clearly.** The Bible never speaks of homosexuality in a positive – or even a neutral – light. Sexual relations between members of the same gender always in Scripture are depicted as sinful. The Bible describes such conduct as "an abomination," "degrading," "unnatural," "shameless," and a "perversion." Those who commit same-sex acts, refuse to acknowledge them as sinful, and reject the call to repentance are outside the kingdom of God.

**3. God's creative intent for sexual relations is good.** God created us male and female, and He designed a unique, complementary sexual union between us in the bonds of heterosexual, monogamous life-long marriage. Summarizing the 2,000-year-old Christian narrative on sexuality and marriage, Pascal-Emmanuel Gobry writes, "The sexual act is meant to reflect God's love by fostering a union at once bodily and spiritual – and creates new life.... The fruitfulness of the marriage act reflects that God is a creator and has charged man to be an agent of his ongoing work of creation. And, finally, if God's love means total self-giving unto death on a Cross, then man and wife must give themselves to each other totally – no pettiness, no adultery, no polygamy, no divorce, and no nonmarital sexual acts."[20]

Genesis 1-2 establishes at least seven norms for marriage: Marriage is covenantal, sexual, procreative, heterosexual, monogamous, non-incestuous, and symbolic of the gospel, according to Denny Burk in *What is the Meaning of Sex?*[21]

**4. Jesus affirms Old Testament teachings about sexuality and marriage.** Matthew 19:1-12 is instructive. The Pharisees confront Jesus after He crosses over the Jordan into Judea and they ask, "Is it lawful for a man to divorce his wife on any grounds?" Rather than debate the lawfulness of failed marriages, Jesus takes the religious leaders back to the Garden of Eden. "Haven't you read," He replies, "that He who created them in the beginning made them male and female ... For this reason a man will leave his father and mother and be joined to his wife, and the two will become one flesh? So they are no longer two, but one flesh. Therefore, what God has joined together, man must not separate."

The Pharisees respond, "Why then did Moses command us to give divorce papers and send her away?" Jesus tells them, "Moses permitted [not commanded] you to divorce your wives because of the hardness of your hearts. But it was not like that from the beginning."

Clearly, the Lord has not changed His reasons for creating men and women, nor has His "divine accommodation" (allowing divorce under terms of the Mosaic Law) lowered His standards for sexual purity and marriage. There is no divine accommodation for homosexual conduct.

**5. Christians share with our homosexual friends a struggle against sinful desires.** Everyone is born with "original sin" – a natural tendency to live independently of God. When we act upon fleshly desires, we violate God's holy standards and are in need of His saving grace. The apostle Paul, quoting from the Psalms, reminds us, "There is no one righteous, not even one; there is no one who understands, there is no one who seeks God. All have turned away, together they have become useless; there is no one who does good, there is not even one" (Rom. 3:10-12). Paul further reminds us in Rom. 3:23, "For all have sinned and fall short of the glory of God," and then he points out both the consequences of our sin and the remedy, "For the wages of sin is death, but the gift of God is eternal life in Christ Jesus our Lord" (Rom. 6:23). Paul even calls himself chief among sinners (1 Tim. 1:15).

Christians are far from perfect. We struggle with sins like lust, anger, lying, selfishness, arrogance, and all other ways humanity rebels against our Creator. Remembering our sinful tendencies helps us see the sins of other people in a more accurate, and gracious, light. Yes, Christians have the Holy Spirit who dwells within us and gives us power over sin. But we often give in to our fleshly desires – and even make excuses such as, "I can't help it," or, "I've always had this weakness." Perhaps the reminder of the beams in our own eyes will help us deal more gently with those suffering from a speck of dust in theirs. This commonality with our gay and lesbian friends makes us vulnerable, but also more genuine and compassionate.

**6. People can change.** Paul makes this clear in 1 Cor. 6:9-11. He begins with a negative: "Do you not know that the unjust will not inherit God's kingdom? Do not be deceived: no sexually immoral people, idolaters, adulterers, male prostitutes, homosexuals, thieves, greedy people, drunkards, revilers, or swindlers will inherit God's kingdom." Then, he reminds his fellow believers, "Some of you were like this; but you were washed, you were sanctified, you were justified in the name of the Lord Jesus Christ and by the Spirit of our God."

The evidence indicates that same-sex attraction typically is discovered early in life and involves a combination of biological, psychological, and environmental factors, and that it tends to stay with us for a lifetime.[22] In other words, an individual with same-sex attraction likely will struggle with that throughout his or her lifetime. The difference is that the one who is in us – the Holy Spirit – is greater than the one who is in the world.

God gives us the ability to overcome even the strongest sinful urges.

Numerous testimonies by formerly gay individuals, and by Christians who acknowledge same-sex attraction but remain celibate, serve as a witness to the transforming power of Christ. Consider, for example, Wesley Hill, assistant professor of Biblical studies at Trinity School for Ministry, and Julie Rodgers, ministry associate for spiritual care at Wheaton College. Both acknowledge same-sex attraction, agree that homosexual and lesbian conduct is sinful, and have chosen to live celibately while serving in positions of Christian leadership.

We should note that the Bible has something to say about celibacy. The Bible undercuts our cultural obsession with sexual fulfillment. Scripture bears witness that followers of Jesus may live full lives of freedom, joy, and service without sexual relations. Matt. 19:10-12 and 1 Cor. 7:1-9, 25-40 commend the celibate life as a way of faithfulness. We should acknowledge the power of sexual drives and subject them to constraints, either through marriage or disciplined abstinence. But never within a Biblical perspective does sexuality become the basis for defining a person's identity or for finding meaning in life. The love of God is far more important than any human love. Sexual fulfillment finds its place, at best, as a subsidiary good within this larger picture. [23]

How do we challenge self-defined homosexual Christians to reshape their identity with the gospel? Despite our culture's view, sexual gratification is not a sacrament and celibacy is not a fate worse than death. Sexual abstinence can promote a life "devoted to the Lord without distraction" (1 Cor. 7:35).

**7. We should welcome into our churches those struggling with same-sex attraction.** This does not mean that those living unrepentant, openly gay lifestyles should be received as members, or should play any role in the leadership of the church. But as Andy Stanley, senior pastor of North Point Community Church in Alpharetta, Ga., noted at a 2015 Catalyst West conference, the local congregation ought to be the "safest place on the planet for students to talk about anything, including same-sex attraction."[24] By extension, the church should be a safe place for anyone struggling with same-sex attraction to have a candid, caring conversation.

We should not deny church membership to those who confess same-sex attraction *and* agree that same-sex lust and conduct are sinful – *and* who seek to overcome these sinful desires and behaviors by the power of God and the accountability of a community of fellow believers. Would we not afford the same consideration to those who struggle with heterosexual lust, gossip, pride, or gluttony? At the same time, we need to be consistent in our stand on Biblical conduct and church discipline. For two people living together outside of marriage, or engaged in adultery, or any other activity the Bible clearly condemns, we need to follow the pattern of church discipline Jesus lays out in Matthew 18 and we see exemplified in other passages of Scripture.

In summary, God has spoken clearly on the issue of same-sex conduct; the Scriptures never speak of it in a positive light – and further, describe it as sinful. God created us in His image and for relationships, and His creative intent for men and women is life-long, heterosexual, monogamous relationships in the confines of marriage, which pictures the relationship of Christ and His church. When tested about divorce, Jesus takes the Pharisees back to God's creative intent for marriage and proper sexual conduct.

Homosexuality is neither a special class of sin nor the unpardonable sin. All of us share fleshly desires, and all of us act on our natural-born tendency to live independently of God. But God did not leave us there. He did something about it. He sent His Son to earth, where He added to His deity sinless humanity, lived a perfect life, and on the cross took our sins upon Himself. Through His death, burial, and resurrection, He conquered Satan, sin, and death for us, and we may receive forgiveness of sins, everlasting life, and the presence of the Holy Spirit, who provides an avenue of escape from the most challenging sinful desires (see 1 Cor. 10:13).

The church should minister to people struggling with same-sex attraction, knowing that some of us were bound in sinful behaviors, but now we are washed, sanctified, and justified. Homosexuality is one form of sexual sin and is no greater or lesser sin than any other, although its bondage may cling more heavily and it may have graver physical, emotional, and relational consequences than other sins. Our Christian brothers and sisters may struggle with varying degrees of same-sex attraction their entire lives – and we should be there to struggle alongside them.

We must live as a community of believers that embraces sinners as Jesus did – demonstrating His humility and sacrificial love and, simultaneously, His divine righteousness. In the midst of a culture that worships self-gratification, and in a church that often preaches a false Jesus who panders to our desires, those who seek the narrow way of obedience have a powerful word to speak.[25]

How different would the issue of same-sex attraction look if the church had always viewed homosexuality as one of the many natural sins to which some people are drawn as a result of living in a fallen world? And what if we had always talked openly about the sexual temptations we all face?[26]

*The Bible expresses the heart of the unchangeable God as He speaks to the rebellious heart of people. While the times have changed, the human heart has not; it continues to be deceitful above all things and desperately wicked.*

# 5

# BUT WHAT ABOUT...

*Commonly raised objections*

Below are some commonly raised objections to the Biblical view of same-sex conduct.

## I WAS BORN THIS WAY

If homosexuality is genetically determined, then we may view it in the same light as race and gender, placing homosexuals in the same protected class as racial minorities and women. This also enables same-sex advocates to paint those who stand against homosexual behavior as oppressors who oppose civil rights. This is a winning strategy, as a Pew Research Center poll discovered, finding a direct correlation between the belief that homosexuality is inborn and support for same-sex marriage.[27]

We may legitimately question the validity of research that concludes the inborn nature of homosexuality, asking whether it has been authenticated and peer reviewed. At the same time, we should understand that the studies address only homosexuality's *origins*, not its normality or morality, according to Joe Dallas, Christian counselor, speaker, and author. Finally, we should be prepared to respond graciously and clearly if studies ever successfully link biology and homosexuality.

The "born gay" argument is based on the belief that what we are is what we were meant to be. But there is much that argues against this. We are imperfect from conception. All of us share in original sin. Some of us have birth defects, or seem naturally inclined to antisocial behavior. Our human natures are fallen and therefore our tendencies only tell us what is, not what ought to be.

Incidentally, the contention that "I was born this way" is not limited to same-sex attraction with respect to human sexuality. A recent *New York Times* article by Richard A. Friedman cites new research showing that some women, like men, are "biologically inclined to wander." Women who carry certain variants of the vasopressin receptor gene are much more likely to engage in "extra pair bonding," the scientific euphemism for sexual infidelity.

While reporting the scientific findings, Friedman is quick to point out two caveats: "Correlation is not the same as causation; there are undoubtedly many unmeasured factors that contribute to infidelity. And rarely does a simple genetic variant determine behavior." And, he asks, "So do we get a moral pass if we happen to carry one of these 'infidelity' genes? Hardly. We don't choose our genes and can't control them (yet), but we can usually decide what we do with the emotions and impulses they help create."[28]

Joe Dallas writes, "David laments that he was born in sin (Ps. 51:5) and Paul confirms both the inborn nature of sin and our ongoing struggle with it (Rom. 6-7). The first human tragedy we see in Scripture speaks to this, as God informs Adam that sin's impact on him and his race will be both spiritual and physical (Gen. 3:17-19; see also Rom. 5:12-20). The sin nature manifests itself from birth and we wrestle with it until death."[29]

Our gay friends may tell us, "I can't help my same-sex attraction; I didn't ask to be this way." This is a wonderful opportunity for us to affirm them as precious people made in the image of God while acknowledging the pervasiveness of sin. Same-sex attraction is one of many manifestations of our fallen nature. At the same time, deliberate, immoral responses to our "natural" desires are acts of rebellion against God and thus both sinful and harmful.

We might also encourage our Christian friends struggling with same-sex attraction by pointing out the beauty of suffering in the Christian life. Though He is God's Son, Jesus "learned obedience through what He suffered" (Heb. 5:8). The apostle Paul writes that his goal is "to know Him and the power of His resurrection and the fellowship of His suffering, being conformed to His death" (Phil. 3:10). After being stoned and left for dead outside Lystra, Paul returns with Barnabus, "strengthening the disciples by encouraging them to continue in the faith and by telling them, 'It is necessary to pass through many troubles on our way into the kingdom of God'" (Acts 14:22). Lastly, Paul writes this to the Romans: "we also rejoice in our afflictions, because we know that affliction produces endurance, endurance produces proven character, and proven character produces hope. This hope does not disappoint, because God's love has been poured out in our hearts through the Holy Spirit who was given to us" (Rom. 5:3-5).

The American Psychological Association defines sexual orientation as "an enduring pattern of emotional, romantic, and/or sexual attractions to men, women, or both sexes." When describing where this attraction comes from, the APA is honest that "although much research has examined the possible genetic, hormonal, developmental, social, and cultural influences on sexual orientation, no findings have emerged that permit scientists to conclude that sexual orientation is determined by any particular factor or factors."[30]

"The bulk of evidence regarding the origin of homosexuality," writes Joe Dallas, "still points to a combination of biological, psychological, and environmental factors as its root.... Whatever its cause, though, homosexual orientation is usually discovered, not chosen."[31]

Desires may be involuntary, but acts are chosen. Dallas notes:

1. Homosexuality, like many sexual or emotional tendencies, seems to appear early in life and remain deeply ingrained over a lifetime; however, although homosexual orientation may not be chosen, homosexual behavior clearly is chosen; thus, those who choose it are morally culpable.

2. "Unchosen" and "unchangeable" do not necessarily mean "inborn." It still is unclear what role genetic, biological, or other factors play in the formation of homosexual desires.

3. "Inborn" does not mean "normal" or "God ordained." Many conditions are inborn, but their origin does not determine their normality or morality. Such determinations require a more substantive standard than the explanation of being "born that way."[32]

Sexual behavior sometimes is relegated to a secondary issue. "I'm not hurting anyone," we might hear. "What I do in the privacy of my home is my business and doesn't affect anything else I do." But behavior – public or private – *is* important, and sexual behavior is no less so.

God's creation of men and women includes His design for pleasure and procreation in sexual union, which later appears as a "type" of God's intimate, passionate commitment to His people (see Isa. 54:5-6; Hos. 2:19-20; Eph. 5:22-33). Homosexual behavior, however, is never mentioned positively in Scripture, while monogamous, life-long unity between a man and a woman is the highest expression of God's intimate intentions for His people.

## STOP JUDGING ME

Because Christians believe the Bible condemns same-sex behavior, defenders of this behavior charge us with "judging" LGBT people in violation of Jesus' words, "Do not judge, so that you won't be judged" (Matt. 7:1). Why are Christians so eager to condemn those engaged in same-sex conduct, yet remain virtually silent on the issue of adultery, or two people living together out of wedlock, or any number of other behaviors contrary to Scripture? Shouldn't we clean up our own act before judging others?

In response, perhaps we should begin by agreeing that many Christians impose double standards when condemning certain types of sins. And we should apologize for any real or perceived vitriol toward our LGBT friends. At the same time, we should challenge our friends' misuse of Scripture. In Matthew 7 Jesus corrects, not all types of judgment, but hypocritical judgment. He gives the brilliantly absurd illustration of someone pointing to a speck of dust in his neighbor's eye, all the while sporting a plank in his own eye.

But we *are* to judge behavior by the Word of God – especially in the church. And we are to speak up on issues of eternal significance. Our speech and our actions, however, should be seasoned with gentleness and respect. Perhaps the following New Testament passages are good reminders to us:

**Matt. 18:15-17**: If your brother sins against you, go and rebuke him in private. If he listens to you, you have won your brother. But if he won't listen, take one or two more with you, so that by the testimony of two or three witnesses every fact may be established. If he pays no attention to them, tell the church. But if he doesn't pay attention even to the church, let him be like an unbeliever and a tax collector to you.

**Gal. 6:1**: Brothers, if someone is caught in any wrongdoing, you who are spiritual should restore such a person with a gentle spirit, watching out for yourselves so you won't be tempted also.

**Col. 3:12-15**: Therefore, God's chosen ones, holy and loved, put on heartfelt compassion, kindness, humility, gentleness, and patience, accepting one another and forgiving one another if anyone has a complaint against another. Just as the Lord has forgiven you, so also you must forgive. Above all, put on love – the perfect bond of unity. And let the peace of the Messiah, to which you were also called in one body, control your hearts. Be thankful.

**2 Tim. 2:24-26**: The Lord's slave must not quarrel, but must be gentle to everyone, able to teach, and patient, instructing his opponents with gentleness. Perhaps God will grant them repentance to know the truth. Then they may come to their senses and escape the Devil's trap, having been captured by him to do his will.

**James 1:19**: My dearly loved brothers, understand this: everyone must be quick to hear, slow to speak, and slow to anger.

## THIS IS THE 21ST CENTURY

As the argument goes, Christians are on the "wrong side of history." The Bible is outdated and needs to be brought up to modern times – or abandoned altogether. After all, the Bible endorses slavery, prohibits eating shellfish, and commands people not to sew two kinds of fabric together. We've advanced beyond these ancient commands, so let's bring Christianity into the 21st Century and stop labeling same-sex orientation as sinful.

Responding, we should note that there are several issues raised here. First, that the Bible is fluid and adaptable to our times. In fact, the Bible expresses the heart of the unchangeable God as He speaks to the rebellious heart of people. While the times have changed, the human heart has not; it continues to be deceitful above all things and desperately wicked (Jer. 17:9). God's standards of holiness remain the same because He remains the same yesterday, today, and forever (Heb. 13:8). That is, His holiness, His divine nature, and His standards of right and wrong are eternally constant.

Second, the charge that the Bible endorses slavery suggests that the person raising this charge is unfamiliar with Scriptural context. The Bible does not endorse slavery as we understand it today. Slavery in Bible times operated much more as indentured servanthood, although where slavery resulted from warfare or other issues, the Bible expresses God's "divine accommodation," recognizing the sinfulness of people and seeking His people to be a light that exposes the sinfulness of the institution. Equally important, passages of Scripture encourage the freeing of slaves (Philemon 15-16) and condemn capturing another human being and selling him into slavery (Ex. 21:16; 1 Tim. 1:10). As Kevin DeYoung notes, "To make it sound like the Word of God is plainly for slavery in the same way it is plainly against homosexual practice is biblically indefensible."[33]

Finally, the argument about shellfish, sewing two kinds of garments together, etc., is addressed in the discussion of Lev. 18:22 and Lev. 20:13. As a brief recap, God gives the Israelites certain actions to carry out as a way of *symbolically* telling them not to get mixed in with the false ways of the nations around them. Israel "wears" certain badges of holy distinction that separate them from the morally and theologically corrupted nations surrounding them. These prohibitions are neither exhaustive nor necessarily permanent in all cases.

## THAT'S JUST YOUR INTERPRETATION

Some argue that the Bible passages addressing same-sex behavior are subject to interpretation. Of recent note is Matthew Vines' book, *God and the Gay Christian*. The author attempts to argue that being a gay Christian in a committed same-sex relationship – and eventually marriage – is compatible with Biblical Christianity. Other self-identified Christian authors have attempted to show that the Bible condemns homosexuality only in certain historic, geographic, or cultural contexts.

We have dealt with alternative understandings of the Bible passages in question earlier in this document and refer the reader to the chapter, "Six key passages" (p. 19). At the same time, we should note that if *any* interpretation of a text can be true, then *no* interpretation is true. The goal of interpretation is to understand the author's meaning, not to read our meaning into the text. Studying the text in its original language; taking careful note of context; understanding the author's purpose and seeing what he has written elsewhere; comparing Scripture with Scripture – all of these are responsible approaches to any ancient text. The primary flaw of those promoting alternative interpretations of the Biblical texts on homosexuality is known as *eisegesis* – imposing bias into a text rather than seeking to let the text speak for itself.

As an example of *eisegesis*, Matthew Vines argues that "Christians who affirm the full authority of Scripture can also affirm committed, monogamous same-sex relationships."[34] Vines' main argument is that the Bible has no category for sexual orientation. So, when the Bible condemns same-sex acts, it is actually condemning "sexual excess," oppression, or abuse, not the possibility of permanent, monogamous, same-sex unions. This view begins with the conclusion that "committed, monogamous same-sex relationships" are part of God's creative intent for men and women, and are therefore good, and then seeks to inflict that view upon the Biblical texts.

But in fact, the Bible nowhere limits its rejection of same-sex conduct to exploitative forms. The prohibitions of Lev. 18:22 and 20:13 are unqualified. Any male who lies with another male has committed an abomination. If homosexual actions were wrong because they were exploitative, why does Lev. 20:13 specify the death penalty for both participants?

Paul is equally unambiguous in Rom. 1:26-27. The reference to lesbianism in verse 26 describes behavior in the ancient Mediterranean world that is not confined to exploitative, abusive roles, or active vs. passive roles. Paul's transition to male homosexuality in verse 27 appears to cast all forms of male homosexuality in the same light. "Had Paul wanted to limit his remarks to pederasty he could have used Greek words that refer specifically to such activity," writes Robert A.J. Gagnon.[35]

Further, Gagnon reports that it is misleading to argue as if Jewish Christian writers had nothing but negative images from which to base their judgment of homosexuality. He cites several ancient Greco-Roman documents that tout the compassionate and beautiful character of same-sex love, including Plato's *Symposium*.[36]

## I CAN'T CHANGE

A popular view promoted today by gay activists is that people either are born gay or not, and they cannot change their orientation. Homosexuality has a genetic component that the writers of the Bible did not realize. So, the argument goes, if the uninformed writers of the Old and New Testament documents had only known about this, they would have changed their tune.

Much has been written in response to this view, some of which has been mentioned earlier in this book. Gagnon summarizes various scientific studies in *The Bible and Homosexual Practice: Texts and Hermeneutics*.[37] Here's a brief synopsis:

- Three studies in the 1990s sought to find a difference in the brains of homosexual and heterosexual people. While some differences were discovered, Neil and Briar Whitehead write, "Science has not yet discovered any genetically dictated behavior in humans."[38] In short, genetic influence on homosexuality is, if existent at all, relatively weak in comparison with family, societal, and other environmental influences.
- In the U.S. the odds of a given child becoming homosexual increase dramatically depending on the social environment. Two cultural markers are urban/

rural and level of education. Homosexuality is more prevalent in urban areas, where there are increased opportunities to engage in homosexual behavior and where there are fewer sanctions against it. As for education, men and women who are more highly educated show a higher percentage of homosexual and lesbian behavior, perhaps in part because educators often encourage them to explore their "true" sexuality. Among those whose level of education does not extend beyond high school, only 1.8 percent of men and 0.4 percent of women identify themselves as homosexual/bisexual. Among college graduates the rates are 3.3 percent of men and 3.6 percent of women.

- Further studies indicate the elasticity of sexual behavior, with some who engage in homosexual behavior early in life transitioning to heterosexual later in life, and vice versa. Gagnon notes, "People who at one time or another experience homosexual impulses do so at different levels of intensity at different times of life, and for periods of different duration.... None of this corresponds to a doctrine of biological determinism."[39]

Can homosexuals change? Yes. Change can take different forms: a reduction in or elimination of homosexual behavior; a reduction in the intensity and frequency of homosexual impulses; the experience of heterosexual arousal and marriage; or reorientation from exclusive or predominant homosexuality to exclusive or predominant heterosexuality.

"It is evident, then, that the genetic or intrauterine component of homosexual orientation is indirect and not dominant," concludes Gagnon. "Indeed, the latest scientific research on homosexuality simply reinforces what Scripture and common sense already told us: human behavior results from a complex mixture of biologically related desires (genetic, intrauterine, post-natal brain development), familial and environmental influences, human psychology, and repeated choices. Whatever predisposition to homosexuality may exist is a far cry from predestination or determinism and easy to harmonize with Paul's understanding of homosexuality."[40]

## IT'S NOT A BIG DEAL

Self-identified Christians who support same-sex conduct may say something like this, "There are only a handful of Bible verses that even mention homosexuality. So, it's not that big a deal."

However, if we believe God's Word is inspired, inerrant, infallible, and sufficient, then every word *is* a big deal. For the Holy Spirit to inspire a single passage makes that passage true, meaningful, and relevant. The importance of a Biblical doctrine is not necessarily tied to the number of times Scripture addresses it. For example, the phrase "1,000 years" is mentioned only six times in Scripture and limited to a single chapter (Revelation 20). Yet volumes have been written about the "millennium," and regardless of one's view of its ultimate fulfillment, all Christians look forward to the day when Christ returns and sets things right.

Further, even though there are only six passages that speak specifically to homosexuality, many other passages complement these verses. Consider, for example, these texts, which include the six primary passages addressed earlier: Gen. 9:20-27; 19:4-11; Judges 19:22-25; Lev. 18:22; 20:13; Ezek. 16:50 (possibly also 18:12 and 33:26); Rom. 1:26-27; 1 Cor. 6-9-11; 1 Tim. 1:9-11; and probably Jude 7 and 2 Peter 2:7. Add to these the texts on cult prostitution: Deut. 23:17-18; 1 Kings 14:24; 15:12; 22:46; 2 Kings 23:7; Job 36:14; and Rev. 21:8 and 22:15.

God has spoken clearly on the issue of same-sex behavior, and His perspective of our response to His creative intent is, well, a big deal. It's also good to keep in mind that when any narrative like the Bible is shared, it's not necessary to retell something that already has been clearly established. As James M. Hamilton Jr., writes, "In other words, as a writer introduces his audience to the world in which his story is set, if he tells them that world includes the earth's gravitational force pulling objects toward itself, he does not have to reiterate that explanation when he shows a plane crash. The author does not need to interrupt the narrative and remind his audience about gravity."[41]

Lastly, when it comes to believers, the Biblical injunctions toward healthy sexuality (and against unhealthy sexuality) are not merely concerned with the private morality of individuals but for the health, wholeness, and purity of the Christian community. Israel is called to be a holy nation for the sake of all nations. Paul's injunction to "glorify God in your body" (1 Cor. 6:20) grows out of his passionate concern for the unity and sanctification of the community as a whole.

As we look at an injunction against prostitution (1 Cor. 6:15), to engage in sexual immorality defiles the body of Christ. Through baptism, Christians have entered a corporate whole whose health is at stake in the conduct of all its members. The New Testament never considers sexual conduct a matter of purely private concern between consenting adults. According to Paul, everything we do as Christians, including our sexual practices, affects the whole body of Christ.[42]

*No one is entirely free to live as they please.*

# 6

# CONVERSATION WITH A GAY FRIEND

*What do you say when the tough questions come?*

A few years ago I joined leaders of a Christian non-profit organization in a meeting with executives of a Nashville, Tenn., TV station. They were preparing to launch a new program catering to the LGBT community. We asked them to reconsider.

Among the TV executives was a lesbian. She wanted to know why Christians couldn't just accept her for who she is. It was the only time I recall speaking up, and I said something like this:

"I accept you for who you are, if you accept me. We are both sinners who struggle with many desires. Some of them are good and some of them are not. The Bible teaches us how to tell the difference. At the end of the day, you and I must decide whether to act on these sinful desires. When we come to the point of losing our shame over sinful behavior – and actually celebrating it – we find ourselves in deep spiritual trouble."

It wasn't the answer she expected. It neither confirmed her suspicion of Christian malice nor compromised Biblical truth. The meeting ended cordially. A few weeks later the station premiered "Out & About."

## BIGOTS AND HATEMONGERS

The experience raised my awareness that many who struggle with same-sex attraction think Christians hate them. Perhaps some Christians do, as evidenced by the self-righteous protestors that stand on street corners and hoist signs saying, "God hates fags."

But they do not represent the Christians I know, who strive to follow the example of Jesus to be soft on people and hard on sin. This is challenging when the people we are called to love cast us as bigots, hatemongers, and hypocrites for opposing their lifestyles.

The apostle Peter urges us to always be ready to give a defense of our faith "with gentleness and respect" (1 Peter 3:15-16). So perhaps this is a good time to rehearse a hypothetical conversation with a gay friend, who asks pointed questions.

**Q: Why do you hate people with same-sex attractions?**
A: Have I said something to give you that impression? If so, I am truly sorry. In fact, if any Christian expresses hatred toward you, they have denied the command of Jesus to love everyone. Jesus loved people enough to speak the truth to them, however. He confronted them about their sin while offering forgiveness. That's something we both need. You and I share a natural tendency to live independently of God. Jesus calls us to repentance and offers us eternal life.

**Q: Jesus never spoke against homosexuality.**
A: Actually, He did. He affirmed God's creation of male and female, along with God's intent for one man and one woman to be joined in marriage for a lifetime (Matt. 19:4-6). Anything

outside of God's design is sin – and that includes all forms of sexual immorality. Jesus also affirmed the truthfulness of the Old Testament, which identifies homosexuality as sinful behavior; and He called Paul, who wrote against homosexuality, to be an apostle.

**Q: I want to marry my partner. What right do you have to stop me?**

A: Don't I have a right to express my views and vote my convictions? Besides, no one is entirely free to live as they please. A man in love with two women is not permitted to marry them both. Eight-year-olds can't obtain a marriage license. And a brother can't marry his sister. The laws respecting the sanctity of marriage – as it is traditionally defined – are based on the state's interest in promoting a familial arrangement whereby a mother and a father raise children that come from their union. The state is in the marriage business for the common good and for the well being of the society it is supposed to protect. While there are individual exceptions, numerous studies confirm that children do better with a mom and a dad, and communities do better when husbands and wives stay together.

**Q: Some day the laws will change – perhaps even this year.**

A: Maybe so, but what is legal is not necessarily what is right. God's standards remain the same because He is a God of supreme holiness who knows what's best for us.

**Q: Who are you to tell me what's right and wrong? The Bible says judge not, doesn't it?**

A: The passage you're referring to is in Christ's Sermon on the Mount and speaks to the issue of hypocritical judgment – focusing on the speck in someone else's eye when I have a plank in my own eye. That's not the same as upholding the unchanging standards of right and wrong found in the Bible – standards Jesus clearly affirmed.

**Q: Am I going to hell?**
A: That's not my call. And it's not God's desire for you.

**Q: You must think homosexuality is the unpardonable sin.**
A: Of course not. But you make a good point. As Christians speak out against homosexuality, we should speak out with equal conviction against adultery, pornography, and other sins that may ensnare all of us. While some sins carry more severe human consequences, all sins grieve the heart of God and led Jesus to the cross, where He bore the penalty for my sins, and yours.

**Q: But I was born this way.**
A: Really? Studies regarding the "gay gene" show that biological processes may influence behavior but do not determine it. Sin comes naturally to all of us. But Jesus offers us victory over sin and will change our desires. The apostle Paul wrote to Christians who once engaged in homosexual acts and other sinful behavior, saying, "Some of you were like this; but you were washed, you were sanctified, you were justified in the name of the Lord Jesus Christ and by the Spirit of our God" (1 Cor. 6:11).[43]

# 7

# WHAT SHOULD CHURCHES DO?

### *Six recommendations for facing an uncertain future*

At this time, nobody knows the degree to which federal and state legislative and judicial bodies will impose the normalization of same-sex conduct on private businesses and religious institutions. However, there is little doubt that public opinion already is pressuring churches to accept same-sex couples as members – and even to celebrate homosexual relationships that are "loving," "committed," and "monogamous." The time may come when the state orders a church not to discriminate in any way for purposes of membership or employment based on "sexual orientation."

Is there anything local congregations should do now to provide legal protection and to prepare for an uncertain future? Consider the following recommendations:

**1.** Be committed to a Biblical understanding of human sexuality and marriage, and proclaim the whole counsel of God – no matter the cost.

**2.** Make sure your church has the broadest religious liberty protections under the law. An excellent free resource is *Protecting Your Ministry: A Legal Guide for Southern Baptist and Evangelical Churches, Schools, and Ministries.* The 40-page booklet is a joint effort between the Ethics & Religious Liberty

Commission of the Southern Baptist Convention and Alliance Defending Freedom. It may be downloaded at erlc.com/store.

**3.** Be a safe place for people struggling with same-sex attraction. This does not mean that those living unrepentant, openly gay lifestyles should be received as members, or should play any role in the leadership of the church. But vibrant, disciple-making local congregations should not deny church membership to those who confess same-sex attraction *and* agree that same-sex lust and conduct are sinful – *and* who seek to overcome these sinful desires and behaviors by the power of God and the accountability of a community of fellow believers. The apostle Paul's testimony of genuine change in the lives of people at Corinth should be an encouragement to all of us (1 Cor. 6:11).

**4.** Be consistent in your stand on Biblical conduct and church discipline. For any two people living together outside of marriage, or engaged in adultery, or any other activity the Bible clearly condemns, church leaders need to follow the pattern Jesus lays out in Matthew 18 and we see exemplified in other passages of Scripture.

**5.** Consider what a gifted academic and committed follower of Jesus, who also struggles with same-sex attraction, says Christians who struggle with ongoing same-sex attraction need from the church: (a) To recognize that "those people" are sometimes sitting in the second row; they desire to be loved, to belong, and to be faithful; (b) to realize that everyone is sexually broken; (c) to be willing to accept struggle – to treat homosexual sex the same way it treats extramarital sex, and to create space for repentance and restoration; (d) to unashamedly share the Scriptural truth that sex is for heterosexual, covenant marriage only; (e) to make room for "baptismal family" – in other words, if we ask gays and lesbians to forgo one kind of intimacy because it is rightly seen as disordered and incompatible with Scripture, then we must come around them to offer the tightest and most beautiful family we have; and (f) to show kindness as Jesus always did with recovering sinners.[44]

**6.** Don't despair. While Christians swim against the tide of public opinion and common practice, we have a divinely appointed opportunity to be salt and light. No whining allowed. Consider first-century Christians, who faced ostracism and intense persecution – not merely for their stand on moral issues but primarily because they loved Jesus and served Him faithfully. As a result, the church grew from 120 on the Day of Pentecost to 30 million by the middle of the 4th Century.

In *The Apology of Aristides the Philosopher*, delivered about A.D. 125 to Caesar Titus Hadrianus, it is noted that Christians, though a harried underclass, "do not commit adultery nor fornication, nor bear false witness, nor embezzle what is held in pledge, nor covet what is not theirs. They honour father and mother, and show kindness to those near to them; and whenever they are judges, they judge uprightly.... And their oppressors they appease and make them their friends; they do good to their enemies ..."[45]

God is able to do all things. He particularly delights in choosing "the world's foolish things to shame the wise, and ... the world's weak things to shame the strong" (1 Cor. 1:27). His power is perfected in our weakness (2 Cor. 12:9). As a humbling reminder, if the Lord can use the mouth of a donkey to speak truth to a false prophet, there's even hope for us (see Num. 22:21-31).

# 8

# FOUR EVANGELICAL APPROACHES

*How Christian views have varied over 50 years*

Evangelicals are anything but monolithic in their views of sexuality and LGBT rights. A study by sociologists Jeremy Thomas of Idaho State University and Daniel Olson of Purdue University, as they combed through nearly 50 years of *Christianity Today* articles on the issue, reveals four basic approaches:

**1. Biblical intolerance:** "The Bible says it's a sin; that's good enough for me." Even in the 1960s, evangelicals acknowledged that being gay isn't a choice – it was seen as a psychological disorder. Still, the Bible speaks clearly on homosexual behavior.

**2. Natural intolerance:** "It's against human nature." In the 1980s, some evangelicals began turning to a new argument that involved health and the natural order. Since many people rejected the teachings of the Bible, this new approach appealed to natural law as the foundation of public morality and the law. This approach was not inconsistent with the Bible but also was not tied directly to it.

**Public accommodation:** "It's a personal sin, but we live in a pluralistic society." A dominant view today is that homosexual behavior is a personal sin, but not a public concern. Evangelicals who espouse this view stand strong on Biblical morality while recognizing that we live in a pluralistic society in which the rights of everyone should be protected. This response generally supports expanded LGBT rights, including job discrimination protections, adoption, and civil unions, but draws a line in the sand on same-sex marriage.

**4. Personal accommodation:** "It's about love and respect, not sex." This is the most recently developed evangelical view. It's a minority view, and some evangelicals warn against this approach as a slippery slope into embracing homosexual behavior as normative. This view emphasizes the love (not sex) between same-sex couples, with no judgment of the morality of these relationships. The Bible is used to argue for equal rights for everyone.[46]

# 9

# WHERE DO THEY STAND ON SAME-SEX MARRIAGE?

## *A snapshot of world religions and denominations*

According to a 2014 article by the Pew Research Center, here's a snapshot of where major religions and Christian groups stand on same-sex marriage:[47]

| Sanctions Same-Sex Marriage | Sanctions Blessing of Same-Sex Unions | Prohibits Same-Sex Marriage | No Clear Position |
|---|---|---|---|
| Conservative Jewish Movement | Episcopal Church | American Baptist Churches | Buddhism |
| Reform Jewish Movement | Presbyterian Church (USA)* | Church of Jesus Christ of Latter-day Saints (Mormon) | Hinduism |
| Society of Friends (Quakers) | | Islam | |
| United Church of Christ | | Lutheran Church-Missouri Synod | |
| Evangelical Lutheran Church | | Orthodox Jewish Movement | |
| | | Roman Catholic Church | |
| | | Southern Baptist Convention | |
| | | United Methodist Church | |

**PUSA has since changed its position and now sanctions same-sex marriage.*

# FURTHER READING

The following resources may help you learn more about same-sex issues from a Biblical perspective.

*What Does the Bible Really Teach about Homosexuality?* by Kevin DeYoung

*The Same Sex Controversy* by James R. White and Jeffrey D. Niell

*God and the Gay Christian? A Response to Matthew Vines,* edited by R. Albert Mohler Jr.

*Why Not Same-Sex Marriage?* by Daniel Heimbach

*The Bible and Homosexual Practice: Texts and Hermeneutics* by Robert A.J. Gagnon

*Same-sex Marriage: A Thoughtful Approach to God's Design for Marriage* by Sean McDowell and John Stonestreet

*The Moral Vision of the New Testament: Contemporary Introduction to New Testament Ethics* by Richard B. Hays

*unChristian: What a New Generation Really Thinks about Christianity ... and Why It Matters* by David Kinnaman and Gabe Lyons

# NOTES

[1] http://freedomtomarry.org.

[2] http://www.theguardian.com/world/2015/may/26/vatican-ireland-gay-marriage-referendum-vote-defeat-for-humanity.

[3] For two views of New McCarthyism see "Rise of the New McCarthyism," http://www.pfaw.org/rww-in-focus/rise-of-the-new-mccarthyism-how-right-wing-extremists-try-to-paralyze-government-throug; and "The New 'McCarthyism' Exists, but It Has Nothing to Do with Ted Cruz," http://www.nationalreview.com/article/415932/new-mccarthyism-exists-it-has-nothing-do-ted-cruz-charles-c-w-cooke.

[4] Sean McDowell & John Stonestreet, *Same-sex Marriage: A Thoughtful Approach to God's Design for Marriage* (Grand Rapids, MI: Baker Books, 2014), 38.

[5] These truths are explored in more detail in *ibid.*, 35-42.

[6] Kevin DeYoung, *What Does the Bible Really Teach about Homosexuality?* (Wheaton, IL: Crossway, 2015), 26.

[7] *Ibid.*, 27-32.

[8] Other passages on God's intention for sexuality include Mark 10:2-9; 1 Cor. 7:1-9; Eph. 5:22-33; 1 Thess. 4:3-8; and Heb. 13:4.

[9] James R. White & Jeffrey D. Niell, *The Same Sex Controversy: Defending and Clarifying the Bible's Message About Homosexuality* (Minneapolis: Bethany House, 2002), 46.

[10] *Ibid.*, 51.

[11] DeYoung, 42-47.

[12] White & Niell, 65.

[13] Paul Copan, *Is God a Moral Monster? Making Sense of the Old Testament God* (Grand Rapids, MI: Baker Books, 2011), 74. See also Gordon J. Wenham, *Leviticus*, New International Commentary on the Old Testament (Grand Rapids, MI: Eerdmans, 1979), 270.

[14] *Ibid.*, 77.

[15] See "The Negative Effects of Societal Endorsement of Homosexuality," Robert A.J. Gagnon, *The Bible and Homosexual Practice: Texts and Hermeneutics* (Nashville: Abington Press, 2001), 471-84.

[16] apa.org/topics/light/orientation.pdf.

[17] Denny Burk, *God and the Gay Christian? A Response to Matthew Vines* (Louisville: SBTS Press, 2014), 48.

[18] Richard B. Hays, *The Moral Vision of the New Testament: Contemporary Introduction to New Testament Ethics* (New York: Harper Collins, 1996), 393.

[19] Burk, 51.

[20] Pascal-Emmanuel Gobry, "Why so many Christians won't back down on gay marriage," *The Week*, online edition, Sept. 3, 2014.

[21] Denny Burk, *What Is the Meaning of Sex?* (Wheaton, IL: Crossway, 2013), 88-106, quoted in *God and the Gay Christian? A Response to Matthew Vines*, 53.

[22] For a fuller discussion of the scientific evidence, see Joe Dallas, "Speaking of Homosexuality," *Christian Research Journal*, Vol. 29, No. 06, 2006; and Robert A.J. Gagnon, *The Bible and Homosexual Practice: Texts and Hermeneutics* (Nashville: Abington Press, 2001), 395-432.

[23] Hays, 391.

[24] Michael Gryboski, "Andy Stanley: Churches Should Be 'Safest Place on the Planet' for Gay Youth," Christianpost.com, April 18, 2015.

[25] Hays, 403.

[26] For more, see Dan Kimball, *They Like Jesus but Not the Church: Insights from Emerging Generations* (Grand Rapids, MI: Zondervan, 2009), Chap. 8, "The Church is Homophobic."

[27] "Public Opinion Trends of Gay Marriage," The Pew Forum on Religion and Public Life, cited in Joe Dallas, "Speaking of Homosexuality," *Christian Research Journal*, Vol. 29, No. 06, 2006.

[28] Richard A. Friedman, "Infidelity Lurks in Your Genes," http://www.nytimes.com/2015/05/24/opinion/sunday/infidelity-lurks-in-your-genes.html?rref=collection%2Fcolumn%2Frichard-a-friedman.

[29] Joe Dallas, "Speaking of Homosexuality," *Christian Research Journal*, Vol. 29, No. 06, 2006.

[30] apa.org/topics/light/orientation.pdf.

[31] Joe Dallas, "Speaking of Homosexuality."

[32] *Ibid.*

[33] DeYoung, 107.

[34] Matthew Vines, *God and the Gay Christian* (New York: Convergent Books: 2014), 3.

[35] Gagnon, 349.

[36] *Ibid.*, 350-361.

[37] *Ibid.*, 395-432.

[38] Neil and Briar Whitehead, *My Genes Made Me Do It! A Scientific Look at Sexual Orientation* (Lafayette, La., Huntington House, 1999), 209.

[39] Gagnon, 418. The author cites numerous studies supporting the elasticity of sexual behavior and the possibility of change on pp. 418-29.

[40] *Ibid.*, 430. The author expands on these comments in a section entitled, "Relation of the Scientific Data to Paul's Views," 430-32.

[41] James M. Hamilton Jr., *God and the Gay Christian? A Response to Matthew Vines*, 29.

[42] See Hays, 391-92.

[43] Rob Phillips, adapted from "Is homosexuality the worst sin?" which appeared in *The Pathway* and Baptist Press in 2013.

[44] Cited in Sean McDowell & John Stonestreet, *Same-sex Marriage: A Thoughtful Approach to God's Design for Marriage* (Grand Rapids, MI: Baker Books, 2014), 153-55.

[45]http://www.earlychristianwritings.com/text/aristides-kay.html.

[46]Tobin Grant, Religion News Service blog, "Corner of Church and State," Aug. 15, 2014.

[47] David Masci, "Where Christian Churches, other religions stand on gay marriage," Pew Research Center, June 18, 2014.

# ADDITIONAL RESOURCES

## *Other books by Rob Phillips:*

### *The Apologist's Tool Kit*

*The Apologist's Tool Kit* equips you to defend the Christian faith "with gentleness and respect" (1 Peter 3:16). The articles in this 81-page booklet address some of the most commonly challenged Christian doctrines today, from the existence of God to the authority of Scripture. In addition, they offer a Biblical basis for identifying and dealing with false prophets, and they provide an overview of several religions, cults, or sects that lay claim to scripture but deny its core teachings.

**Order online at mobaptist.org/apologetics.**

### *The Kingdom According to Jesus: A Study of Jesus' Parables on the Kingdom of Heaven*

Jesus used more than a dozen parables to reveal previously hidden truths about the kingdom of heaven, but for many the kingdom remains a mystery. What is the kingdom of heaven? Is the kingdom here, or are we to wait for it? Who's in the kingdom and who's not? And what can we learn from Jesus' stories of mustard seeds, pearls and bridesmaids? *The Kingdom According to Jesus* explores these questions in a simple and compelling way that encourages readers to "seek first the kingdom of God" (Matt. 6:33).

**Available from Amazon and other booksellers.**

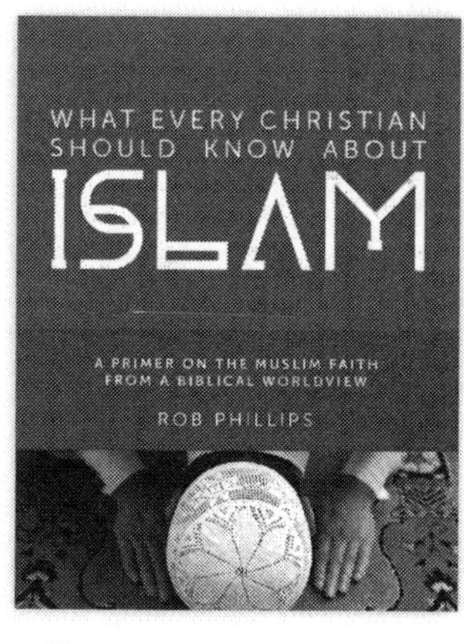


## *What Every Christian Should Know About Islam:*

*A Primer on the Muslim Faith from a Biblical Worldview*

The world's 1.6 billion Muslims are precious people for whom Christ died. At the same time, Islam is a false religion that enslaves people and strives for global conquest. *What Every Christian Should Know About Islam* offers a brief overview of this 1400-year-old religion and answers key questions about the religion of Muhammad from a Biblical perspective.

**Order online at mobaptist.org/apologetics.**

**Kindle edition available from Amazon**.

## *Web resources:*

Visit the Missouri Baptist Convention's apologetics webpages at **mobaptist.org/apologetics**.

View, download, and share apologetics resources at **oncedelivered.net**.